S0-ADZ-513

WITHDRAWN

3 1526 03854497 6

WITHDRAWN

Properties of Materials

Shiny or Dull

Charlotte Guillain

Heinemann Library
Chicago, Illinois

www.heinemannraintree.com
Visit our website to find out more information about Heinemann-Raintree books.

To order:

☎ Phone 888-454-2279

🖳 Visit www.heinemannraintree.com to browse our catalog and order online.

© 2009 Heinemann Library
an imprint of Capstone Global Library, LLC
Chicago, Illinois

Customer Service: 888-454-2279

Visit our website at www.heinemannraintree.com

All rights reserved. No part of this publication may be reproduced or transmitted in any form or by any means, electronic or mechanical, including photocopying, recording, taping, or any information storage and retrieval system, without permission in writing from the publisher.

Designed by Joanna Hinton-Malivoire
Photo research by Tracy Cummins
Printed and bound by South China Printing Company Ltd

13 12 11 10 09
10 9 8 7 6 5 4 3 2 1

Library of Congress Cataloging-in-Publication Data

Guillain, Charlotte.
  Shiny or dull / Charlotte Guillain.
    p. cm. -- (Properties of materials)
  Includes bibliographical references and index.
  ISBN 978-1-4329-3288-6 (hc) -- ISBN 978-1-4329-3296-1
(pb) 1. Surface roughness--Juvenile literature. 2. Materials--
Texture--Juvenile literature. I. Title.
  TA418.7.G8558 2008
  620.1'1292--dc22
                            2008055120

Acknowledgments
The author and publishers are grateful to the following for permission to reproduce copyright material: Alamy p. **18** (© foodfolio); © Capstone Publishers p. **22** (Karon Dubke); Corbis pp. **5** (© Fancy/Veer), **20** (© Frithjof Hirdes/zefa); Getty Images p. **8** (Gavin Hellier/Robert Harding); Photolibrary pp. **9** (Frazer Cunningham/Mode Images), **11** (Corbis), **13** (Yves Regaldi/Zen Shui), **15** (Creatas/Comstock), **16, 23** top (Chuck Pefley/Tips Italia), **19** (Yoav Levy/Phototake Science); Shutterstock pp. **4** (© Christopher Elwell), **6** (© garloon), **7, 23** bottom (© Sailorr), **10** (© Rafal Olechowski), **12** (© Tony Sanchez-Espinosa), **14, 23** middle (© Mike Flippo), **17** (© Marie C. Fields), **21** (© OkapiStudio).

Cover photograph of skyscrapers reproduced with permission of Shutterstock (© Serp). Back cover photograph of a yoyo reproduced with permission of Shutterstock (© Mike Flippo).

The publishers would like to thank Nancy Harris and Adriana Scalise for their assistance in the preparation of this book.

Every effort has been made to contact copyright holders of any material reproduced in this book. Any omissions will be rectified in subsequent printings if notice is given to the publisher.

Contents

Shiny Materials

Some things are shiny.

Shiny things can be smooth.

Shiny things can be hard.

Light makes shiny things shine a lot.

Dull Materials

Some things are dull.

8

rough

smooth

Dull things can be smooth or rough.

Dull things can be hard or soft.

Light makes dull things shine a little.

Shiny and Dull Materials

Rock can be shiny. It can be smooth.
It can be hard.

Rock can be dull.

It can be rough. It can be hard.

13

Plastic can be shiny.

It can be smooth. It can be hard.

14

Cotton can be dull.

It can be rough. It can be soft.

15

Metal can be shiny.

It can be smooth. It can be hard.

16

Paper can be dull.

It can be smooth. It can be soft.

shiny

You cannot feel if something is shiny or dull.

shiny

You can see if something is shiny or dull.

You can see a shiny thing is smooth.

You can see a dull thing is rough.

Quiz

Which of these things are shiny?
Which of these things are dull?

22

Picture Glossary

metal hard, shiny material

plastic material that can be soft or hard

shiny bright. Shiny things reflect light.

23

Index

Note to Parents and Teachers
Before Reading
Tell children that you can see if an object is shiny or dull. Shiny things can be smooth and hard, and light makes shiny things shine a lot. Dull things are not shiny. Dull things can be smooth, hard, and light makes them shine only a little. Show children pictures of shiny and dull materials. Let children guess which materials in the pictures are shiny or dull.

After Reading
Give children a bag of objects. Ask them to decide which objects are shiny or dull. Have children feel the objects and decide if they are hard or soft, or rough or smooth. When they are done sorting, have children turn and talk to a partner. Have them discuss the objects. Ask children if their partner sorted objects in the same way that they did. What do their objects have in common? How are they different?